HEERESGESCHICHTLICHES MUSEUM in VIENNA

Published in collaboration
with the Army Museum
Text by Liselotte Popelka

120 Colour illustrations

Vertrieb
für Österreich
VERLAG STYRIA, Schönaugasse 64
A 8010 GRAZ

für die Bundesrepublik Deutschland
VERLAG STYRIA, Schillerstrasse 6
D 5000 Köln 51

Via Cairoli 18/b
50131 Florence (Italy)
Telex 571323 CEB

Printed in EEC by
Centro Stampa Editoriale Bonechi

Translation by
Erika Pauli, Studio Comunicare

ISBN 3-222-11761-6

CONTENTS

Facade of the Museum with sandstone statues by Hans Gasser (1817-1868). Under the round windows, female allegories of Force, Justice, Religion and History; below, the male statues of Valor, Allegiance to the Flag, Sacrifice and Military Intelligence.

Frontispiece: the Arsenal from the northwest. In the foreground one of the porticoes with artillery; in the background the building which houses the museum.

INTRODUCTION

The collections of the Army Museum (Heeresgeschichtliches Museum, literally Museum of the History of the Army) are among the oldest state collections in Vienna. The material initially included pieces that had been brought together in the old Imperial Arsenal of the Innere Stadt as early as the 17th century.
In the 18th century this unique and interesting ensemble became even more fascinating when the Hapsburg collection of parade armature was transferred from the Stallburg to the arsenal in 1750 and, together with the trophies taken in the wars against Frederick II of Prussia, was decoratively installed on the walls and ceilings. The old arsenal however was more than just a storehouse for memories of glorious events and personalities. It was also an arms depot, where pieces were repaired and could be drawn upon in case of a general mobilization.
The events of 1848, above all the assault, capture and sack of the arsenal by the revolting citizens (October 7th), led in the autumn of 1848 to the decision to build the Imperial Royal Artillery Arsenal on a height to the southeast and outside of Vienna. Built as a fortress with an arms depot, barracks and living quarters for the officers, this imposing military complex (a rectangle measuring 688 meters), now the seat of the Arsenal, was one of the major architectural undertakings realized by the young emperor Francis Joseph in the early years of his reign. More than 177 million bricks were transformed into 31 buildings, at a cost of more than eight and a half million florins. The creation of a splendid autonomous museum building in this context was the merit of the Danish architect Theophil Hansen (1813-1891). It was built in the course of only a few years (from 1850-1856) and at the time was without peer in Vienna.
The mixture of styles - Byzantine, Gothic and Hispano-Moresque - corresponded to the concept of dignity the building was expected to manifest. Inside, a central hall with a dome gave it an almost religious character. The pictorial decoration is on the same elevated level.
The allegorical paintings by Karl Rahl (1812-1865) above the windows of the staircase symbolize Strategy, Stories of War and Tactics, and those in the ceiling vault Wile and Courage, Power and Union, Fame and Honor, while those in the Hall of Honor illustrate important events in Austrian history from the Babenbergs on. The four large reinforcing

arches contain frescoes of the Battle of Nördlingen (1634), the Council of War in Occasion of the Battle of Saint Gotthard on the Raba (1664), the Battle of Senta (1697), and the Liberation of Turin from the Siege (1706). The adjacent hall on the left contains episodes from the reign of Maria Theresa and Joseph II up to the taking of Belgrade in 1789. On the right are the Napoleonic wars from the battle of Würzburg in 1796 to the Tyrolean struggle for independence of 1809, up to the negotiations for the armistice between Field Marshal Radetzky and Victor Emmanuel II, King of Sardinia, after the battle of Novara in 1849. All these frescoes are the work of Karl von Blaas (1815-1894) whose realistic colorful painting was more to the emperor's liking than that of Rahl. This tendency of the monarch to favor scientific exactitude and historical fidelity is also apparent in the way in which material transferred to the Arsenal from 1856 on was exhibited. In 1869 the collection was opened to the public, and the first catalog appeared that same year. But when the new Kunsthistorisches Museum on the Ring was terminated in 1881, all the imperial collections of art were gradually transferred there, including, in 1888, the collection of arms belonging to the private patrimony of the Hapsburgs. At this point the only thing left in the Arsenal was the war material that belonged to the State and which was administered by the artillery depot.

Thought however had already been given to a museum dedicated exclusively to the imperial army. At the beginning, from 1885 on, a commission under the sponsorship of the hereditary prince, Rudolf, took matters in hand. The artillery general Archduke William and the famous patron Count Hans Wilczek were also members of the commission. What the munificence of the emperor and the members of the ruling family had put together was integrated by acquisitions and bequests on the part of officers and many private citizens, as well as the results of an ordinance which made it obligatory to hand over to the museum the weapons and flags no longer in use and the honors conferred on the Knights of Maria Theresa who had died. When the Heeresmuseum (literally Museum of the Army) was inaugurated on May 25, 1891 by the emperor Francis Joseph, it truly presented "a coherent picture of the internal and external evolution of the development of the Austrian Army" with its chronologically arranged exhibitions of weapons, uniforms and gear, its trophies and "relics". A room dedicated to guns and one to artillery had been installed on the ground floor. The latter contained above all models of cannons from the 16th century on. The imposing series of Austrian and foreign cannons was set up outside, in front of the museum. The closure of the Army Museum from the summer of 1914 to 1921 as a result of World War I did not in the least put a halt to museum activities. What really happened was that the

Room of the generals seen from the museum entrance. In the room, 56 life-size marble statues of supreme commanders of the army decorate the piers.

The emperor Francis Joseph I (1830-1916)

ALBRECHT ADAM (1786-1862) and FRANZ ADAM (1815-1866).
Oil on canvas, 392 x 346 cm., 1856.

The young monarch is portrayed in a landscape near Vienna; in the background, glimpses of cavalry and artillery. At the corners of the elaborate frame are the coats of arms of Bohemia, Hungary, Old Austria, and Lombardy-Venetia.

museum became a center for the collection of historically interesting war materials and of works by artists who recorded their impressions at the front. Thus in 1923 a gallery of war paintings was inaugurated on the first floor. In 1934, on the ground floor, two rooms reserved for the front on the Isonzo were added.
During World War II the museum remained open at first and, in the service of war propaganda, prepared exhibitions dealing with the various fronts. It was partially destroyed in the bombings of September 1944 and most of the museum pieces transferred there in the last year of the war were destroyed or pillaged. Even so the threatened closure of the museum after the end of the war was averted and in 1955 the reconstruction of the building had on the whole been concluded.
The losses suffered in the war, the change in the historical situation and the absence of an Austrian federal army up to the peace treaty of 1955 led to a change in the museum's name and installment policies. It was now possible, in the Heeresgeschichtliches Museum (literally Museum of the History of the Army), through suitable installations, to stress the esthetic values of the objects and set them in a wider cultural-historical setting, thanks to the inclusion of paintings and sculpture collected in the period between the two wars and augmented by loans. The farsighted request made by Lieutenant General Tiller in his memorandum to the museum in 1883 was thus fulfilled. All that remains of the original aspect of the rooms of the old Museum of the Army is the color red and the restoration on the shields in the vaults of the first room, where the table showcases designed by Theophil Hansen are also still in use. The depots next to the ex-command of the Arsenal, destroyed in the aerial bombardment in 1944, have been replaced by porticoes, in which, well protected, the greater part of the precious artillery collection has been installed. The naval section is an important addition from after the end of World War II, and was made possible only thanks to the models of Austrian warships that were ceded by the Technisches Museum. Today the armored craft currently in use by the Federal Austrian army is on display behind the museum.
The Heeresgeschichtliches Museum has gathered together "what different peoples have accomplished in a wide range of fields: military art, industry and commerce, the arts, research. It becomes evident, more here than elsewhere, that the European peoples constitute a community with the selfsame destiny... Its contents are the best possible publicity for Europe" (H. Zatschek). The poet Reinhold Schneider was deeply moved by the collection "How can one help but be grateful", he wrote in 1958, "to these imposing evocative collections, which will remind our descendants what war was?"

Staircase with the sculptural Allegory of "Austria" (Marble, 1869) by Johannes Benk (1844-1914).

Dome of the Hall of Honor with frescoes by Karl von Blaas (1815-1894).

Hall of Honor with frescoes by Karl von Blaas. In the foreground, part of the mosaic pavement of 1859 (design by Theophil Hansen, 1856).

FROM THE BEGINNINGS OF THE IMPERIAL ARMY TO THE TREATY OF KARLOWITZ (1699)

The room dedicated to the 17th century transports the visitor to a period in European history characterized by two great conflicts: at the beginning of the century, the contrast between Protestant and Catholic countries which came to a head in the Thirty Years' War (1618-1648); in the second half of the century, the struggle against the Turks who were bent on conquering the West.
Added to this was the attempt made by France under Louis XIII and Louis XIV to limit the hegemony of the Hapsburgs in Spain and in the German countries and to make France the leading European power. On the one hand this led to a decades-long conflict with Spain, and wars of conquest on the eastern French frontier; on the other, to alliances with the Turks. England and Holland became more and more important as new powers which had to be reckoned with in Europe, from the point of view of economics as well. Just before the Thirty Years' War, during the struggle for independence of the Netherlands, the "military reform of the Orange" took place. Thanks to expert training in the use of arms and maneuvers, even small armies were better able to resist and outmaneuver the expert Spanish troops. This new technique of fighting spread throughout the north German area and was also adopted by the Swedes, who from 1630 on, under King Gustavus II, known as Gustavus Adolphus, took part in the war in Germany. The Swedish king, head of the Protestant princes, however fell near Lützen in Saxony in 1632 (see page 12). His leather breast plate was one of the most important trophies of the Thirty Years' War in the old Army Museum, until it was sent back to Stockholm in 1920 as a sign of thanks on the part of the Austrian Republic for the "Swedish aid" at the end of World War I. The armaments and methods of combat in that period can be studied from the quantity of weapons, life-size figures of soldiers, and paintings which reveal the predominant part played by the infantry, composed of pike-men armed with long pikes, harquebusiers, and musketeers. The heavy cavalry was composed essentially of cuirassiers and harquebusiers, later replaced by dragoons.
The complete lack of homogeneity in these armed corps was also due to the fact that the men were enlisted only for a specific military campaign. Not until around the end of the 17th century did the protracted length of the campaigns against the Turks require the presence of a certain number of contingents in active service even during the winter. This is the beginning of the so-called standing army which was recruited by the emperor or the provincial states. The unrelenting financial straits of the emperor however made it impossible to arm, equip and assist these troops in a truly unitary way and their number therefore constantly varied.

This situation is what lies behind the importance and influence of the so-called "contractors" who anticipated the money and who saw to the enlistment and outfitting of the soldiers, under their personal responsability, and who therefore succeeded in marshalling a hitherto unimaginable number of troops. On the other hand the power and influence they thus acquired was politically undesirable. Wallenstein, one of the best known figures in military history, is an example of the power, the rise and tragic end of one of these contractors. Twelve large battle paintings by the painter Peeter Snayer of Antwerp, ordered by General Ottavio Piccolomini, illustrate, from a bird's eye view, the way war was carried out in the 17th century, as well as furnishing precious source material on the historical and cultural aspect of life in the fringes of the enormous army of the Thirty Years' War.

The survey of the period, which ended in 1648 with the peace of Westphalia, is completed by one of the swords of Emperor Ferdinand III, who led the army of the Catholic League to victory in 1634 at Nördlingen, and pieces that belonged to General Tilly, one of the League's most important military leaders.

Armor for infantry

(the so-called "foot servants"), in use between 1555 and 1580.

On the left, armor for a non-commissioned officer with more elaborate decoration. In the back, a 16th-century halberd.

22
23
10
11

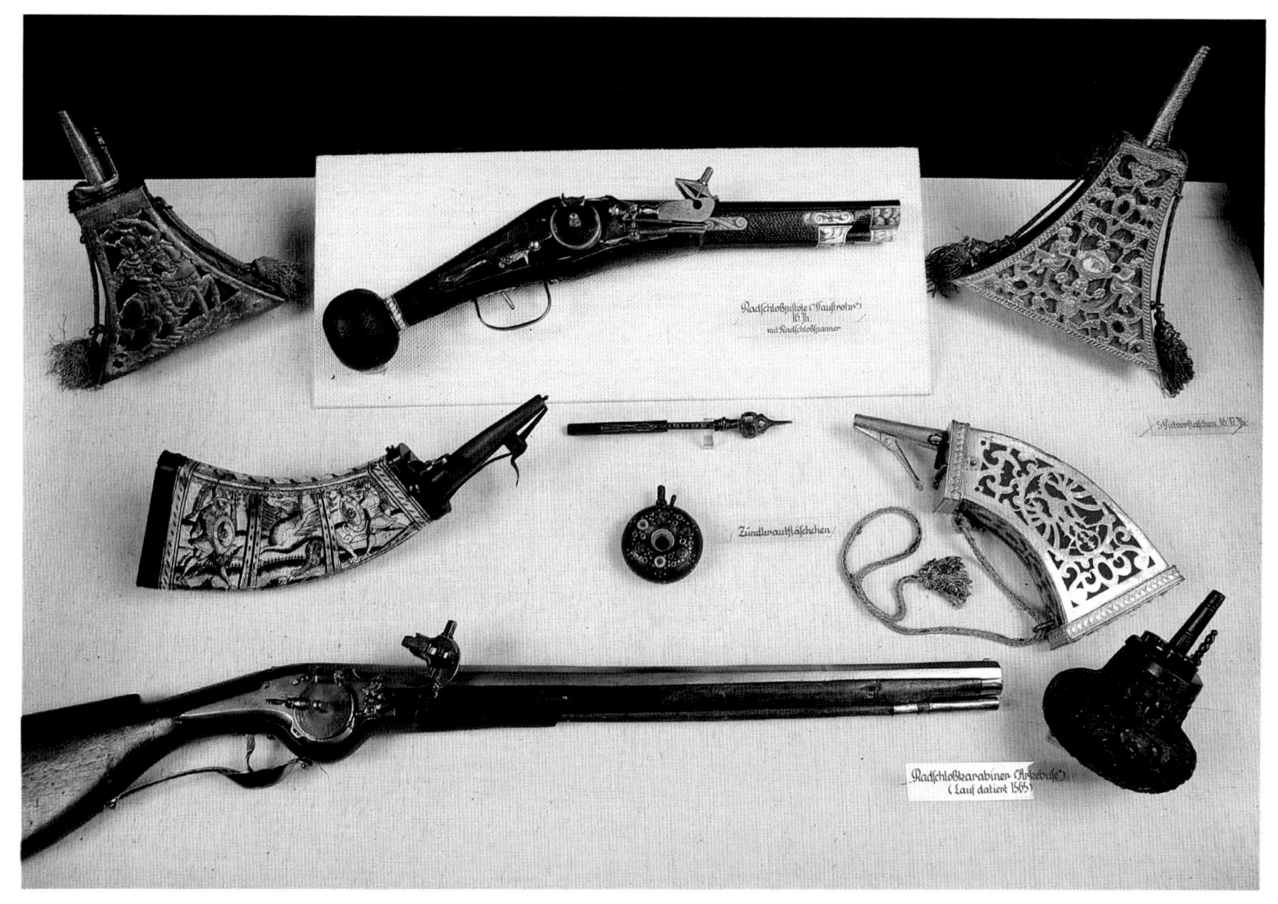

Arms and Accessories

Second half of the 16th and 17th centuries

Above: small wheel-lock harquebus with turnbuckle; below: wheel-lock harquebus.
Powder flasks in metal, wood, horn, leather; at the center a small powder flask.

Emperor Ferdinand III (1608-1657)

JONAS SUYDERHOLF (+ 1686) after P. SOUDTMAN
Etching, 39,9 x 26,3 cm.

As king of Bohemia and Hungary, Ferdinand commanded the imperial forces after the death of Wallenstein; emperor from 1637 on, he sought for peace (1648).

Rifle Drill, ca. 1600

JAKOB DE GHEYN (1565-1629)
Engraving, ca. 1600

Harquebusiers (above) and musketeers (below). The pictures are taken from "Waffenhandlung von den Rören, Musquetten und Spiessen" The Hague, 1608.

Battle before a Besieged City

Dutch school
Oil on canvas, 99 x 146 cm, ca. 1640

Imperial musketeers and pike-men with field scarves fight against the cavalry in the foreground, using their characteristic weapons as prescribed by Gheyn.

Gustavus II, known as Gustavus Adolphus, in the Battle of Lützen of November 6, 1632

Pieter Meulener (1602-1654)
Oil on panel, 49 x 79 cm.

The Swedish king, Gustavus Adolphus, riding a white horse and girded with the blue scarf of full dress uniform, is struck by an imperial cuirassier and falls.

Wallenstein's letter of orders to Pappenheim (Nov. 15, 1632)

Paper, one sheet, 290 x 190 mm.

With this letter the supreme commander of the imperial forces, Albrecht Wallenstein, duke of Mecklenburg (who signed here as AHzM), ordered General Count Heinrich Pappenheim to join him as soon as possible at Lützen with all his troops.

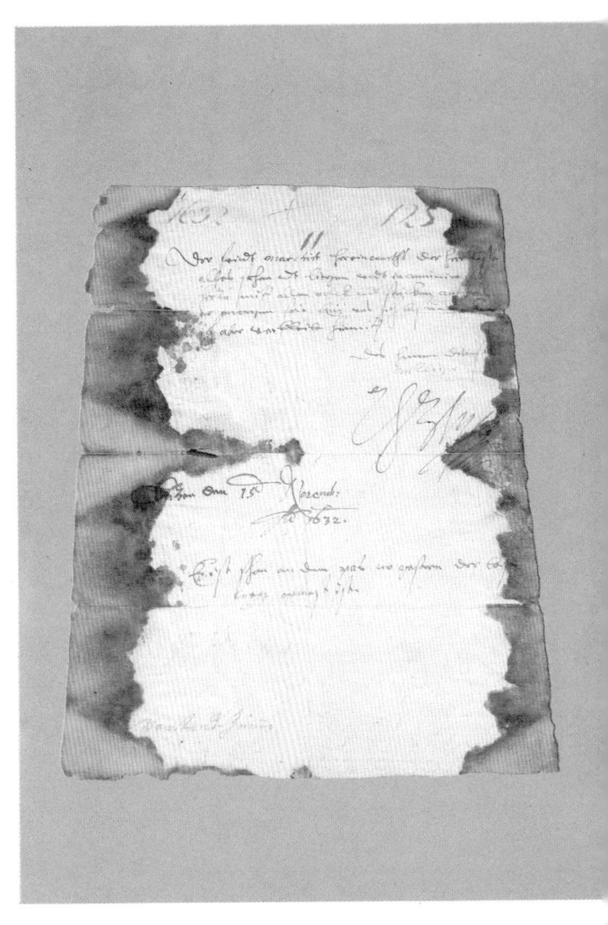

The Assassination of Wallenstein at Eger on February 25, 1634

German school
Tempera on paper, 34 x 52.5 cm., early 19th cent.

Archduke Leopold William (1614-1662)

PAULUS PONTIUS (1603-1658)
Engraving

The archduke Leopold William, one of the brothers of Emperor Ferdinand III, was commander in chief of the imperial forces from 1639 to 1642 and from 1644 to 1645. The engraving shows him in the role of Grand Master of the Teutonic Order; the decoration also makes reference to his role as patron.

Field cuirass of Count Johann Sporck (1601-1679)

Overall height ca. 146 cm., weight 3.8 kg., ca. 1640

General Sporck was one of the most famous cavalry commanders in the Thirty Years' War; he distinguished himself in Tuttlingen, Donau (south of Prague) (1634), Jankau (1645) and above all in the battle of Saint Gotthard on the Raba against the Turks (1644).

Turkish standard (Sanjak)

Red and green silk, 30 x 190 cm, ca. 1683

The central part of this banner, captured in 1683 before Vienna, contains the Islamic creed "There is no god but God, and Mohammed is his prophet"; on the border are verses 1 and 6 of the 48th sura (chapter) of the Koran (victory sura).

Case for the plume from a janissary's headdress

Gilded silver, ht. 30 cm., 17th cent.

The typical headdresses of the special Turkish corps of the Janissaries were decorated with splendid egret plumes which were kept in richly decorated cases.

Turkish timepiece with calendar

Made by the artisans WANIEK AND RAABE (their names are on the back of the timepiece).
Oval case in silver, 6 x 5.3 cm., South German, mid-17th century

The face, decorated with floral ornaments, marks the hours, the day of the month and the phases of the moon, while the names of the months and the days of the week are in the hollows. According to Turkish calculations of time, the timepiece marks August the first, 1664, the date of the battle of Saint Gotthard on the Raba in which it was taken by the imperial troops.

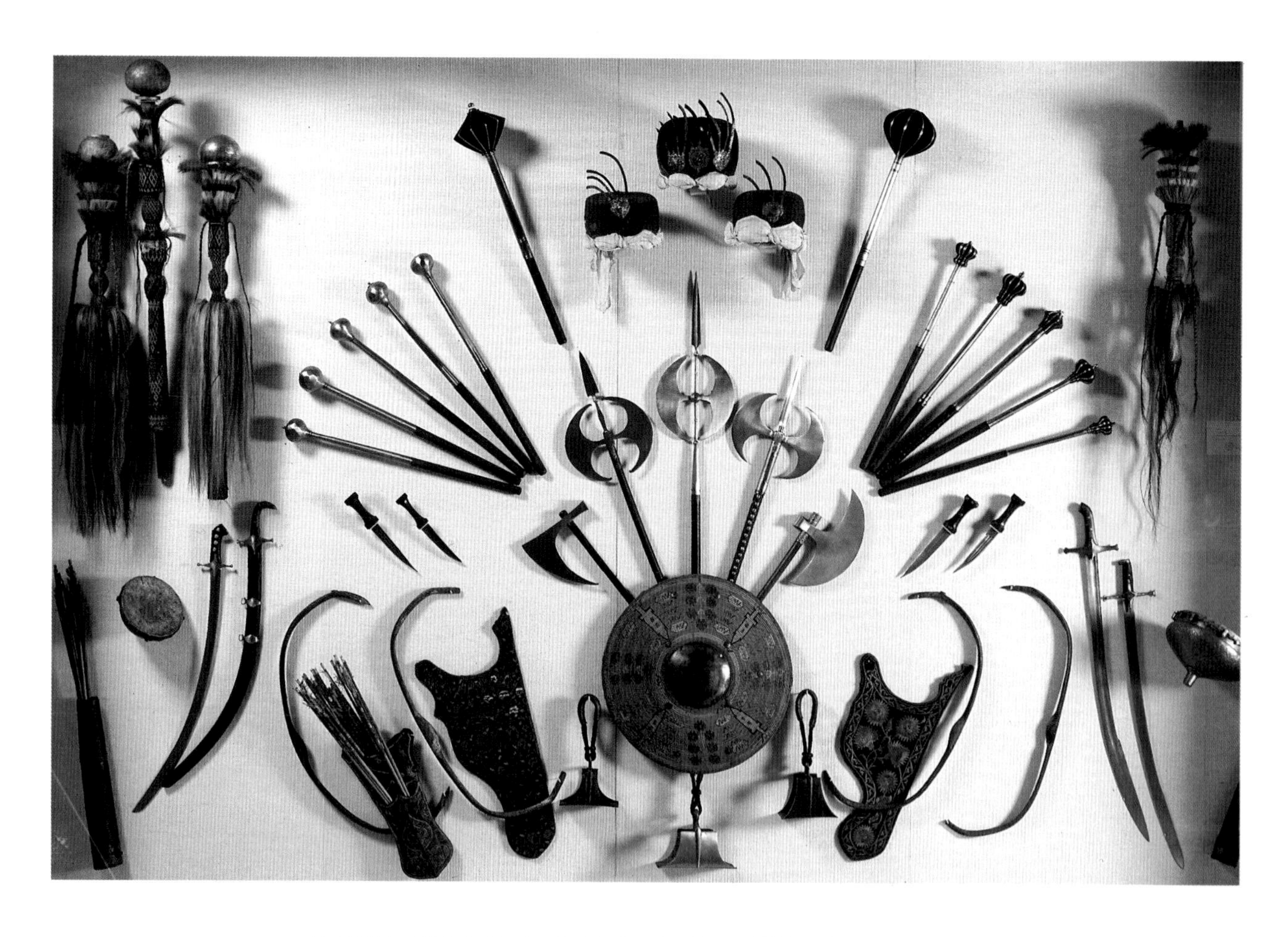

THE WARS AGAINST THE TURKS

The Turks, the enemy against whom the imperial armies - now much more cohesive and better organized - had to fight in the second half of the 17th century, were completely different. Feared for their unusual weapons (above all their composite Turkish bows), their unusual war strategy could be effectively countered only through the use of lighter more manageable arms, and a greater mobility. The victory obtained against the Turks at Saint Gotthard on the Raba on August 1, 1664, was merit of General Count Raimund Montecuccoli, who was particularly influential in Prince Eugene's time, first as a military theoretician and then as president of the Court Council of War. An entire showcase in the museum is reserved for the general. The portrait and armature of the cavalry general Count Johann Sporck are also on exhibition. He too fought at Saint Gotthard on the Raba *(see p. 14).*

The decisive battle against the Turks took place in 1683. In the 17th century, the gigantic Ottoman empire extended over Asia Minor, the Near East and northern Africa, while in the north it included all the Balkans up to Hungary, where the large unsatisfied landholders allied themselves more than once with them against the Hapsburgs, legitimate lords of the country.

When, in July of 1683, Turkish troops commanded by the great vizier Kara Mustafa advanced all the way to Vienna, all of Europe felt threatened. The liberation of the imperial capital with the lifting of the siege, thanks to the military guidance of King Charles of Lorraine and the supreme command of the Polish king John Sobieski, was the prelude to the battle against Turkish Hungary and a splendid triumph. The museum has on exhibit relics of the defender of Vienna, Count Ernst Rudiger von Starhemberg, as well as objects testifying to the reconquest of Ofen and of Belgrade, and a portrait of Louis William, Margrave of Baden, the "Louis of the Turks".

It is thanks to the military genius of Pringe Eugene of Savoy, who was commander in chief from 1697 on and who defeated the Sultan Mustafa II at Senta on the Timis once and for all in that same year, that the Treaty of Karlowitz (1699) was signed, and the greater part of Hungary and all of Transylvania was reacquired. It is therefore fitting that the zone which commemorates Prince Eugene of Savoy (1633-1736) is to be found in the passage from the first to the second room. The concept of Europe was inseparable from that of absolute loyalty to the three emperors this great soldier of fortune served. With his military successes and his capacities as a statesman, he laid the foundations for the status of a great power which Austria conquered in the first three decades of the 18th century. His life span ranged from the 17th to the 18th century and this is why two tokens of his action are also displayed in the room dedicated to the 18th century: the "mortar of Belgrade" and the audience tent of the Turkish grand vizier, in which, in 1716, Eugene wrote his message of victory to the emperor Charles VI after the battle of Peterwardein (northwest of Belgrade). The engravings set on rotating stands also bear the record of the victories won in the war for the Spanish succession in Italy, southern Germany and the Netherlands.

Arms and weapons taken from the Turks

17th century

The showcase contains "horsetails", turbans, hobnailed cudgels; at the center: axes, two-edged axes and daggers; below: sabers, composite Turkish bows in horn with quiver, stirrups, a shield in fig bark, a canteen and a tambourine. The so-called "horse tails" (horsehair of various colors mounted on inlaid poles) were symbols of rank, and the number indicated the honor accrued (the sultan for example had nine tails, the grand vizier five).
The silver plaques attached to the turbans were not ornaments but signs of valor.

Siege and Liberation of Vienna in 1683

Austrian school
Oil on canvas, 236.5 x 389.5 cm., late 17th cent.

This large painting, perhaps commissioned by a general of the empire, presents the two events of the siege and liberation contemporaneously. In the background, the last assault launched by the besieging Turkish troops on September 6, 1683, against the Löwelbastei; in the middle ground and foreground, the battle of liberation of September 12th. The liberating army pours down from the Kahlenberg and each contingent can be identified by its banner: at the center, the imperial troops (standards with the two-headed eagle); in front of them, the Bavarians; in the foreground, the right wing with the Polish cavalry and King John III Sobieski, the supreme commander, at their head on a white dappled horse.

Emperor Leopold I (1640-1705)

Austrian school
Oil on canvas, 233 x 174 cm., ca. 1700

The second son of Emperor Ferdinand III, Leopold, had been destined for an ecclesiastic career but upon the death of his older brother Ferdinand IV he became the successor to the throne for the Austrian hereditary lands and in 1658, emperor. Dedicated to peace and the arts, Leopold was however constrained to fighting many wars; his greatest success was the victory over the Turks and the reconquest of Hungary (1699). As time went on however, the emperor was incapable of taking a firm stand against the claims advanced by Louis XIV of France on the Rhine and in Spain.

Emperor Charles VI (1685-1740)

Austrian school
Oil on canvas, 254 x 166 cm., ca. 1720

As the younger son of the emperor Leopold, Charles was proclaimed king of Spain as Charles III in 1703, after the extinction of the Spanish Hapsburgs, but was unable to retain the land and throne in the war of Spanish succession (1701-14). When his brother Joseph I suddenly died, he inherited the Austrian hereditary lands and the title of emperor. In the war against the Turks of 1736-39, most of the Balkan lands conquered in Prince Eugene's victories of 1716-17 were lost. It was the price which Charles VI had to pay to the European powers for their recognition of the Pragmatic Sanction (female succession) of 1713.

Prince Eugene of Savoy (1633-1736)

JOHANN GOTTFRIED AUERBACH
Oil on canvas, 315 x 237 cm.

In the service of the empire from 1683, in 1697 Eugene obtained the supreme command of the army in Hungary, and in 1701 in Italy. In 1703 he became president of the Court Council of War. His most famous victories were achieved together with the duke of Marlborough in the war of the Spanish succession and in the war against the Turks in 1716-17 (see pp. 20, 21, 23).

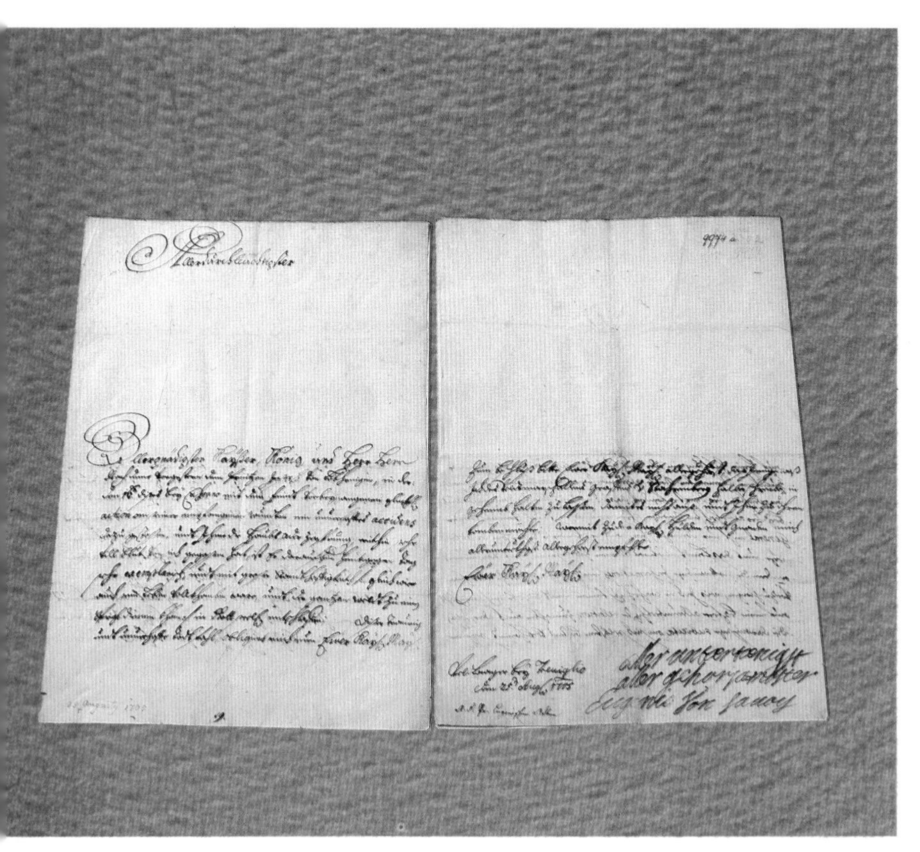

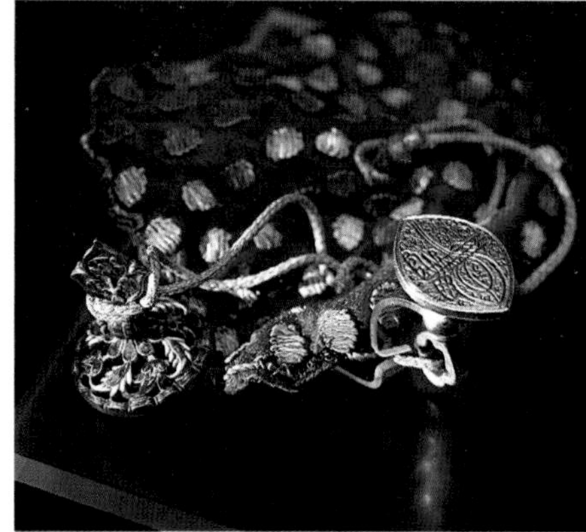

Seal of the sultan Mustafa II

Turkish manufacture
Brass, ht., 3 cm., impression of seal: 1.9 x 2.6 cm., 1695

The pointed oval of the seal bears the various names of the sultan (the tughra) artistically interlaced with the words "Mustafa, son of Mehmed Han, always victorious" and underneath the date of his accession to the throne (1695). The seal was taken during the battle of Senta on the Tisza on September 11, 1697.

Report of Prince Eugene to Emperor Joseph I

Paper, six sheets, military encampment near Treviglio, 25/8/1705

After the battle of Cassano (east of Milan) Eugene reports the death of Prince Joseph of Lorraine, proposes two new regiment commanders, asks for reinforcements and also describes the situation in Piedmont. The young emperor followed Eugene's suggestions.

Funeral decoration for Prince Eugene of Savoy

Austrian make
Black silk velvet with an inset of a cross in gold brocade, 444 x 321 cm.

Coat of arms embrodered in gold on a support in relief, 1736. The pall and the wall hanging behind it (724 and 454 cm.) were probably used in the solemn funeral rites for Prince Eugene in a Viennese church. On the banners, next to the Sabaud coat of arms, are the names and dates of his battles, from Senta (1697) to Belgrade (1717).

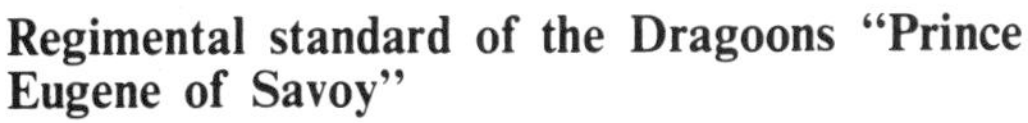

Regimental standard of the Dragoons "Prince Eugene of Savoy"

Red silk brocade, 53 x 79 cm., pole 253.5 cm., 1711-1712

On the front, the interlaced initials of Emperor Charles VI, CRI (Carolus Romanorum Imperator); next to them, embroidered in gold, the inverted initials EVS of the commander of the regiment, Eugene of Savoy. Both sets of initials are also on the point in gilded brass. This standard is one of the oldest insignias of the imperial army extant.

Grenades in glass and drills of the grenadiers

Dark green glass, diam. 10 cm., 18th cent.

Behind are three drawings in India ink by Georg Philipp Rugendas (1666-1742) which show how the grenadiers inserted the fuse in the grenades.

Vertical 10-pounder mortar

LEOPOLD HALIL
Cast in bronze, caliber 17 cm., weight of the barrel 153 kg., about 1714-1738

In the central part, the two-headed imperial eagle with the monogram of Emperor Charles VI ("CVI"). On the left (engraved later), the fortress of Belgrade hit by a shell; to the right, half-bust portrait of Prince Eugene. The inscription records that a small shell from this mortar hit the powder house of the Turkish fortress in Belgrade on the 14th of August 1717.

Part of a Turkish tent

Polychrome silk appliqué on unbleached canvas, 370 x 813 cm., 17th cent.

This part may have been used as roofing. The tent shown on the following page is, according to tradition, that of the grand vizier Dahmad Ali and was taken as booty in 1716 in the battle of Peterwardein. The muskets in the foreground, 17th century, have Miguelet obturators.

ROOM OF MARIA THERESA

(18th Century up to 1790)

By following a clockwise itinerary this room leads from the war of Spanish succession (1701-1714) to the war agains the Turks of 1716-17, up to the battles Maria Theresa (1717-1780) had to undertake as queen of Bohemia and Hungary to defend her hereditary lands. With an army that after the death of her father Charles VI and of Prince Eugene was poorly armed and uncoordinated, Maria Theresa confronted the strong military power of Frederick II's Prussia. Even so the great and beloved sovereign managed to achieve military victories (as witnessed by examples of the booty taken from the Prussians, above all flags) thanks to her advisors and strategists, Daun, Lacy and Laudon, and in 1748 to begin the reorganization of the army.

The objectives were to achieve a uniformity of regulations, insignia, weapons and uniforms for the infantry and the cavalry. While pearl gray had already been used for the uniforms of the infantry from the time of Prince Eugene, after 1748 white became the characteristic color of the rank and file and after 1767 also that of the so-called "German" cavalry (cuirassiers, dragoons). Even so the armies recruited from the various countries of the imperial crown retained their typical national characteristics (see also p. 26). The variety in Maria Theresa's army is also mirrored in 56 watercolors, probably painted by the archduchess Maria Cristina.

Her attention to the army earned Maria Theresa the nickname of "Mater Castrorum". The Military Academy she founded in 1752 in Wiener Neustadt still today trains the officers of the Austrian federal army, and the Military Order of Maria Theresa, instituted in 1757 in memory of the battle of Kolin, was the highest military honor the monarchy could bestow until 1918. Apart from the unique fact that the candidate had to present an eye witness to his act of courage, it must be stressed that this order was also open to officers who were not of noble rank on whom the title of baron was conferred together with the decoration. While these acts were aimed at improving the formation and aspect of the officials, the dynastic concept of Maria Theresa led, after the end of the Seven Years' War, to the transformation of the Imperial Arsenal into a monument that celebrated the dynasty. A series of watercolors demonstrate the changes that took place between 1763 and the middle of the 19th century.

At the time of the co-regency (1742-79) of the emperor Joseph II, the uni-

forms were further standardized and various technical innovations were introduced into the sector of armaments (special arms for each contingent). A special showcase in one of the corners of the room is reserved for hand arms and portable fire-arms in the 18th century. Joseph II's predilection for military uniforms is obvious from his portraits. Moreover, with the creation of the honorary commemorative medal (see p. 31) this enlightened sovereign also succeeded in arousing an awareness of his own worth in the private soldier. The taking of the Turkish fortress of Belgrade by the 71-year-old general Laudon in 1789 was a remote event - way down in Turkey - for Europe as a whole and not only for Goethe. The contemporary French revolution on the other hand marked the beginning of a new epoch. And the room on the other side of the museum, corresponding to that of Maria Theresa, is dedicated to the French Revolution.

The battle of Saragossa of August 20, 1710

JEAN PIERRE BREDAEL (1683-1735)
Oil on canvas, 171 x 257 cm.

This victorious battle of King Charles III's allies against the army of Philip V of Anjou was one of the last imperial successes in Spain. In the middle ground is Charles himself on horseback, in the foreground, the general Count Guido von Starhemberg, commander in chief; to the left, the wounded general of the division Count Hamilton is carried off the field.

Emperor Francis I (1712-1764) and his consort Maria Theresa, queen of Bohemia and Hungary (1717-1780)

School of MARTIN VAN MEYTENS
Oil on canvas, 81 x 64 cm., ca. 1745.

These two portraits meant as pendants show the imperial couple at the time of the first conflict with Prussia.

The battle of Kolin of June 18, 1757

AUGUST QUERFURT (1697-1761)
Oil on canvas, 118 x 187 cm.

The bird's eye view lets the painter illustrate the movements of the troops as if this were a small-scale model. This type of representation and the detailed caption undoubtedly correspond to a desire of the patron. Maria Theresa defined General Daun's victory against Russia at Kolin as the "day the monarchy was born".

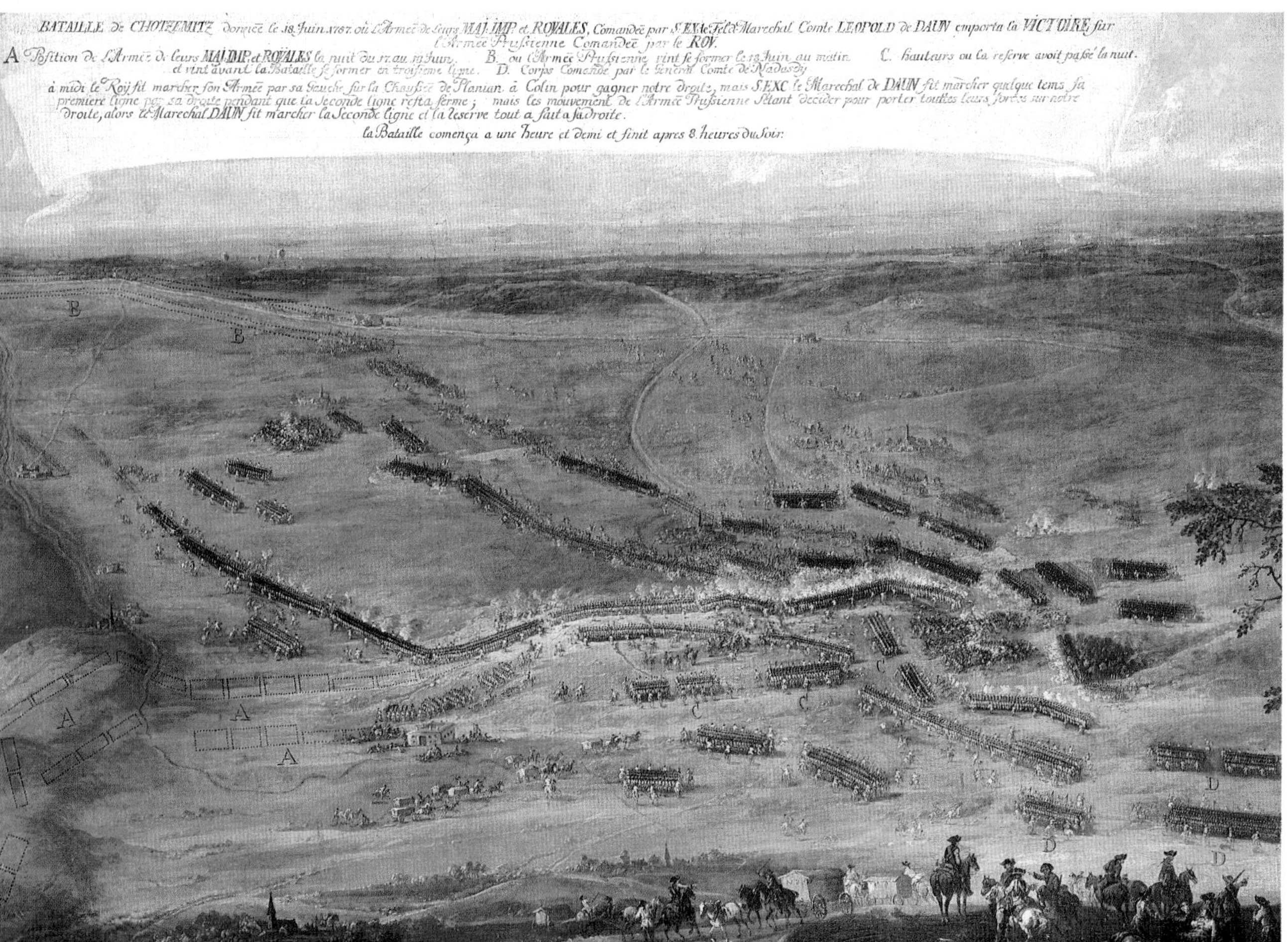
BATAILLE de CHOTZEMITZ donnée le 18 Juin 1757 où l'Armée de leurs MAJ. IMP. et ROYALES, Comandée par S. EX. le Fel. Marechal Comte LEOPOLD de DAUN emporta la VICTOIRE sur l'Armée Prussienne Comandée par le ROY.
A Position de l'Armée de leurs MAJ. IMP. et ROYALES la nuit du 17 au 18 Juin. B. ou l'Armée Prussienne vint se former le 18 Juin au matin. C. hauteurs ou la reserve avoit passé la nuit. et vint avant la Bataille se former en troisieme ligne. D. Corps Comandé par le General Comte de Nadasdy
à midi le Roy fit marcher son Armée par sa Gauche sur la Chaussée de Planian à Colin pour gagner notre droite, mais S. EXC. le Marechal de DAUN fit marcher quelque tems sa premiere ligne par sa droite pendant que la Seconde ligne resta ferme; mais les mouvement de l'Armée Prussienne étant decider pour porter toutes leurs forces sur notre droite, alors le Marechal DAUN fit marcher la Seconde ligne et la reserve tout a fait a sa droite.
la Bataille comença a une heure et demi et finit apres 8 heures du Soir.
A
B
C
D

Cavalry swords and saber sheaths

Period of Maria Theresa.

The saber sheath below, left, dates to 1743-45.

Auxiliary troops at the time of the War of Austrian Succession

MARTIN EENGELBRECHT (1684-1756)
Colored engravings, ca. 1742

Scotch drummer boy and piper, Croation foot soldier.

The Prussians lay down their arms after the battle of Maxen (Saxony) of November 21, 1759

HYACINTH DE LA PEGNA (1706-1772)
Oil on canvas, 260 x 344 cm., 1762

Near Naxen, General Daun captured an entire corps of the Prussian army commanded by General Finck, and the event was mockingly called the "capture of the finch" (in German Fink means finch). The Seven Years' War had not yet come to an end when Maria Theresa commissioned the painter de La Pegna of Brussels to illustrate the most important battles of the war in large paintings.

Field Marshal Count Leopold von Daun (1705-1766)

JOHANN GOTTFRIED HAYD (1710-1776)
Mezzotint, 52.2 x 34.1 cm., 1758

Von Daun distinguished himself in the war between Slesia and Prussia and in 1754 became field marshal. In 1758 he was decorated with the Great Cross of the Order of Maria Theresa for the victory at Kolin. When he reorganized the army he proposed the foundation of what was to become the Austrian Academy. In 1762 he was president of the Court Council of War.

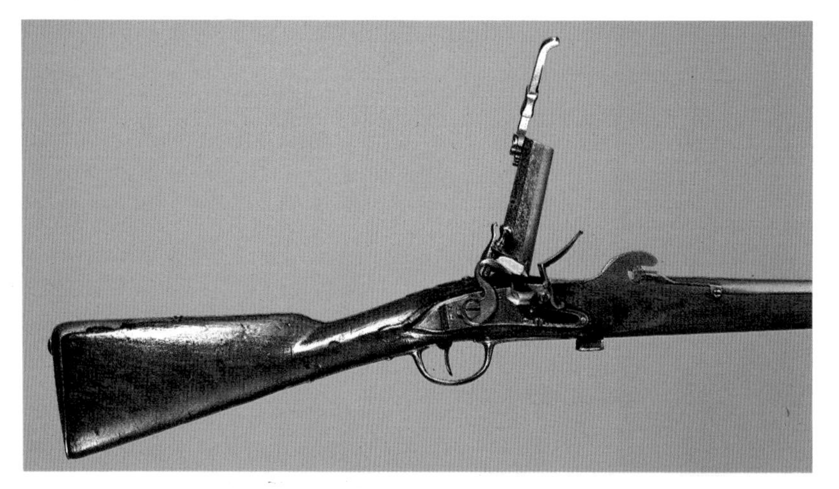

Carbine, model 1770, Crespi system

These arms, transformed according to the invention of the Milanese gunsmith Giuseppe Crespi, were the first breech-loading guns to be used by the Austrian army.

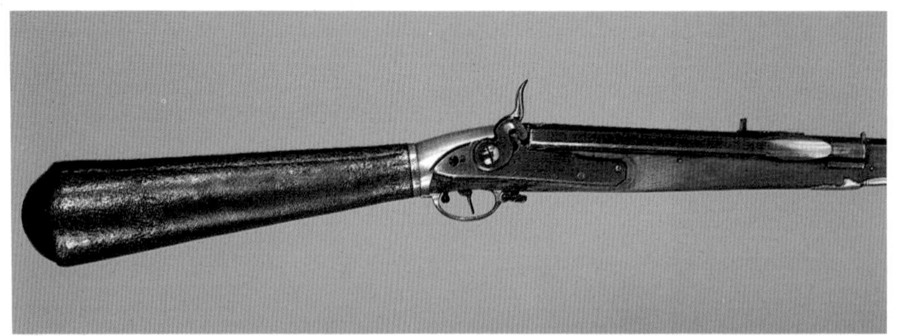

Repeating air rifle, model 1780, Girandoni system.

This breech-loader with a tube magazine and an iron air tank could fire 20 shots in 30 seconds, thanks to the compressed air.

Booty taken from the Prussians in the Seven Years' War.

In the background: grenadier and rifleman caps; next to them, cavalry swords with, in front, two drums taken in 1760 at Londestout in Saxony, and silver bugles made by Blanvalet in Berlin in 1721.

Turkish muskets

18th century

Taken when Belgrade was captured in 1789. The intarsia on the barrel and the stock are evidence of the skill of the Turkish artisans.

Great Cross and Star of the military order of Maria Theresa

Worn in 1759 by the field marshal Baron Gideon von Laudon.

Prussian banners and grenadier's headgear

18th century

Felt caps with the front in embossed brass: in the foreground an officer's neckband.

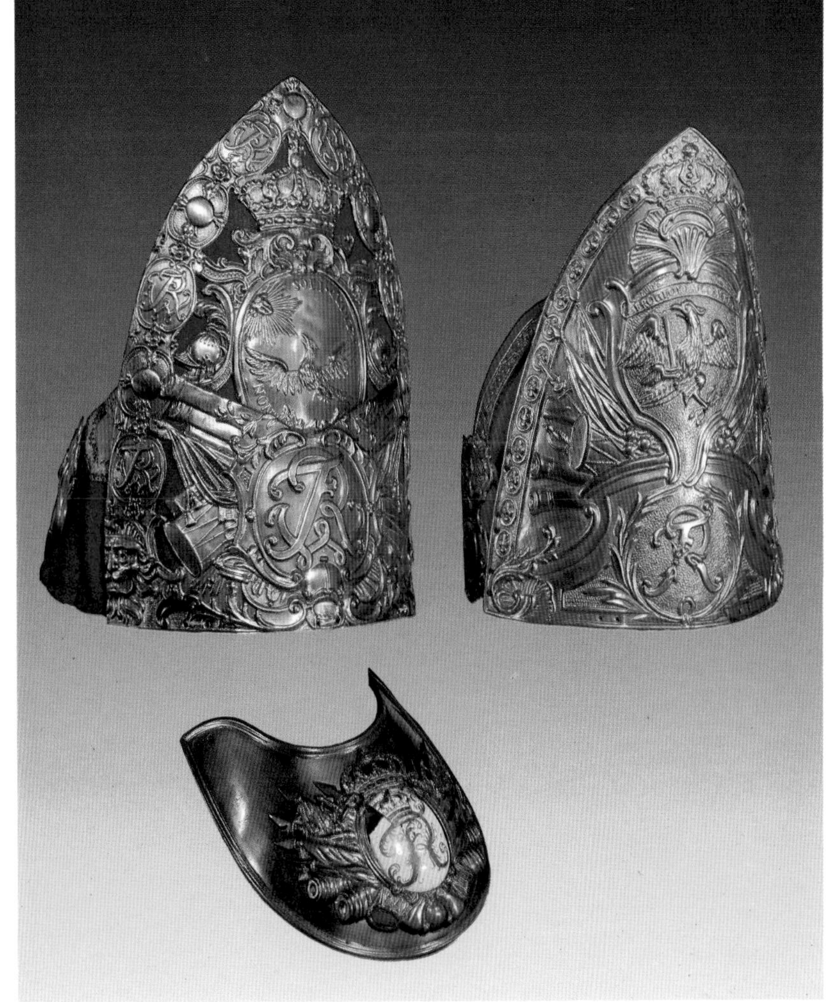

Emperor Joseph II in the Encampment at Minkerdorf

MARTIN-FERDINAND QUADAL (1736-1808)
Oil on canvas, 212 x 325 cm., 1788

The emperor with the archduke Francis and with his generals, including Laudon, Lacy and Hadik, reviewing the troops in 1786 near his summer residence of Laxenburg in Lower Austria, south of Vienna.

Field marshal Laudon on horseback on the battlefield of Kunersdorf

SIGMUND L'ALLEMAND (1840-1910)
Oil on canvas, 370 x 291 cm., 1878

In the course of the Seven Years' War, Baron Gideon Ernst von Laudon (1717-1790), one of the four great generals of Maria Theresa and her son Joseph, inflicted a grave defeat on the Prussian king Frederick II at Kunersdorf on August 12, 1759. The defeat however was not conclusive in deciding the war in Austria's favor.

Commemorative medal of honor

Silver

This honor, instituted by the emperor Joseph II on July 19, 1789, as a "commemorative medal of honor" for non-commissioned officers and privates, was the first of its kind.

Cuirassiers on foot and on horseback

JOHANN CHRISTIAN BRAND (1722-1795)
Oil on panel, ca. 29,7 x 18.1 and 28.8 x 26.8 cm.

In each of these four paintings the painter represents the cavalry in the time of Maria Theresa in the style of the copper engravings. The splendid landscapes serve as background for an accurate reproduction of the equipment.

Cadets in training doing balancing exercises

BERNHARD ALBRECHT (1758-1822)
Tempera on paper, 39.9 x 56.9 cm.

Albrecht taught drawing at the Military Academy of Wiener Neustadt, founded by Maria Theresa, and portrayed the cadets during their military and sport training.

THE FRENCH REVOLUTION AND THE NAPOLEONIC WARS UP TO 1814

(Room of the archduke Charles)

The room, at the center of which is an equestrian statue of Archduke Charles, embraces the years from the French revolution to the fall of Napoleon, when Austria, together with England, Russia and, for a brief period, Prussia, had to withstand the hegemonic intentions of France.
This is the epoch in which the rights of man and of the citizen are proclaimed in France, but in which terror is immediately advocated and applied as a means of government. The emperor Leopold II's sister, Marie Antoinette, also fell as one of its victims. In Napoleon's first campaign, France attacked Austria: the French advancing towards southern Germany were defeated by Archduke Charles, one of the brothers of the emperor Francis II, at Amberg and Würzburg in 1796 (see p. 37), but the young ambitious general Napoleon Bonaparte conquered Lombardy and Mantua and aimed at the heart of Austria. Numerous flags of the revolutionary French armies and the Ligurian and Cisalpine armies document these battles. Carried away by his military successes, Napoleon first proclaimed himself "consul for life" and then had himself crowned emperor of the French in 1804 and King of Italy in 1805. Thus, at the height of his glory, (see p. 34) he made his victorious entrance into Vienna in December, 1805.
In answer to the French challenge, on August 4, 1804, Emperor Francis II, taking the name of Francis I, associated the hereditary title of emperor of Austria with that of the Holy Roman Empire.
Evidence of this is a flag (on the right side of the room) on which, for the first and last time, the crown of the Holy Roman Empire appears above the imperial crown of Austria. Two years later, on August 6, 1806, the emperor Francis II was forced by Napoleon to lay down the dignity of the Holy Roman Empire. The overwhelming success of the French, above all in Napoleon's first campaign, terrified all of Europe. In France, the constitution of the National Guard and wholesale conscription had led to new tactics characterized by rapidity and mobility, which combined a mass attack with the fire of the marksmen in open order, as had been used in the American war for independence. The old linear tactics of the allies were futile against an attack of this type. Despite this, the commander in chief, Archduke Charles, succeeded in defeating Napoleon, who up to then had been thought invincible, at Aspern on May 22, 1809.
This moral success - together with the fact that the prince personally spurred on his troops in the front lines - led to many paintings of this battle. One of these, the enormous

painting by Peter Krafft, was given by the citizens of Vienna to the House of the Disabled (Invalidenhaus). The new bourgeois spirit coming to the fore in Europe was reflected in two other paintings by Krafft, in which the conscript becomes the protagonist in a monumental representation.
The treatises on military theory written by the archduke Charles, who was president of the Court Council of War from 1801 on and who reorganized the Austrian army, are exhibited, together with his Military Order of Maria Theresa and various portraits, in the following commemorative area.

Napoleon I King of Italy

ANDREA APPIANI (1754-1817)
Oil on canvas, 98.5 x 74.5 cm., 1805

Napoleon nominated the Milanese artist Appiani his court painter and he had himself portrayed, at the height of his glory, as king of Italy. He wears the crown made for the occasion and the Order of the Iron Crown which he instituted.

Napoleon's Overcoat

Greyish brown cloth, length 132 cm.

According to tradition Napoleon wore this coat of a Russian officer over the uniform of an Austrian general from the 25th to the 27th of April, during his trip from Fontainebleau to exile on Elba.

The Allies surpass the Vosgi in their march towards France

PETER JOHANN NÖCHLE (1790-1835)
Oil on canvas, 229 x 315 cm.

After the defeat of Napoleon at the battle of Waterloo, south of Brussels, (June 16, 1815), the armies of the Austrian and Russian allies surpassed the Vosgi early in July, 1815, as they advanced into France.
The group in the center shows the emperor Francis I on horseback and the hereditary prince Archduke Ferdinand: behind them is field marshal Prince Schwarzenberg, in front of them the chancellor Metternich. The painter Höchle, from Munich, took part in the advance and sketched the event in only four hours.

Flag of the Lombard Legion, 1797

Green, white, and red silk, embroidered, 143 x 145 cm., pole 163 cm.

This flag of the first cohort of the Lombard Legion (instituted in 1797) is one of the military insignia of the Cisalpine Republic (also created in 1797) and was taken from the Italian troops who were fighting under French command during the Napoleonic wars.

Andreas Hofer (1767-1810)

Attributed to JOHANN GEORG SCHEDLER (1777-1866)
Watercolor on silk, 16 x 12.5 cm.

The portrait of the hero of Tyrolean independence is based on the model the painter and engraver Schedler had used in his etchings from 1809 on. The letter Hofer is writing is addressed to the captain Valentin Tschöll.

Private's uniform, Imperial Regiment of the Hussars of Wurm (later no. 8), prior to 1798

Shako, fur dolman, dolman, trousers: coarse cloth, late 18th cent. Arms: Hussar's carbine, model 1798; Hussar's saber.

The beaker of Olmütz

HANS KELLNER (1582-1617)
Gilded silver, ht., 64.5 cm. After 1600

In 1783, during the first Napoleonic war, this beaker with its richly decorated lid was offered by the city of Olmütz to Emperor Francis II as a volontary contribution for the war. As was the case with other equally precious works of art, this beaker was not melted down but kept in the Imperial Treasury (Schatzkammer) in remembrance of the spirit of sacrifice of the population.

French war balloon

Silk, almost spherical, diam. 9.9 m. Wooden basket, covered with blue canvas: ht., 105 cm.; length 114 cm.

This controlled balloon was captured by the Austrian troops after the battle of Würzburg on September 3, 1796. It is probably the "Intrepide", one of the six balloons used by the French army between 1794 and 1799 for aerial reconnaissance.

Archduke Charles with his children on the Weilburg of Baden near Vienna

JOHANN NEPOMUK ENDER
(1793-1854)
Oil on canvas, 272.5 x 318.5 cm, 1832

The archduchess Maria Theresa (to the left of her father) married King Ferdinand II of the Two Sicilies, the archduke Albert (to the right) as field marshal won the battle of Custoza in 1866, Frederick (on the outer right) was commander in chief of the Austrian navy. Weilburg took its name from Charles' wife, Henriette of Nassau-Weilburg, whose bust appears on the left.

Archduke Charles in the Battle of Aspern

JOHANN PETER KRAFFT (1780-1856)
Oil on canvas, 327.5 x 285 cm., 1812

Krafft represents the famous episode of the battle of Aspern, when Archduke Charles himself carried the standard of the 15th Infantry regiment. The painter shows the Austrian conqueror in a pose similar to that used by J.L. David for Napoleon (Bonaparte at the Great Saint Bernard). The ceramic stove next to the picture comes from Charles' study.

The Return of the Soldier

JOHANN PETER KRAFFT (1780-1856)
Oil on canvas, 280 x 360 cm., 1820

Impressed by the wars against Napoleon, in 1813 Krafft had painted "The Departure of the Soldier". In 1820 he painted this companion picture at the emperor's request. The soldier is decorated with the medal of valor. The two paintings, which introduce genre painting of Biedermeier style, stress the importance of volontary enlistment in the fight against Napoleon.

Announcement of Victory after the Battle of Leipzig on October 18, 1813

JOHANN PETER KRAFFT (1780-1856)
Oil on canvas, 440 x 6.80 m., 1817

The commander in chief of the allied armies, field marshal Prince Charles of Schwarzenberg (1771-1820) announces the victory over Napoleon to the allied sovereigns, Alexander I king of Russia, Francis I emperor, and Frederick Wilhelm III of Prussia. The picture, painted in nine months as a companion piece to the picture of the battle of Aspern, was unveiled on October 18, 1817, anniversary of the "battle of the peoples", in the hall of honor of the Invalidenhaus in Vienna, where a great number of patriots came to see it every year.

Show casket containing the Cross of the Army of Emperor Francis I

Gilded bronze lined with red velvet, on the lid insignias and coats of arms

The Cross of the Army, instituted by Francis I (II) on May 31, 1814, after the first peace of Paris, was to be cast from the metal of the cannons taken from the enemy and conferred on all the participants in the wars against Napoleon. The Cross of the Army which belonged to the emperor and those of his allies, King Frederick William III of Prussia and Czar Alexander II were sent to the old arsenal after their owners had died.

FROM THE CONGRESS OF VIENNA TO THE BATTLE OF SADOWA (1814-1866)

The period from 1814 to 1866 is illustrated in the next long hall, known also as Radetzky Hall after the man who was undoubtedly the best known field marshal in the 19th century. The visitor will find more than Radetzky's personal mementos and the honors bestowed on him, for the room provides above all a precise and effective picture of the Austrian imperial army in the first half of the 19th century. Underlying the forms of a peaceful, almost contemplative, Biedermeier style, expressed in the many genre paintings, scenes of parades and miniature portraits, one can intuit the important function the army must have had as a factor of order and stability in the time of Metternich and the European Restoration.

In 1815 Napoleon was defeated and exiled to Saint Elena. He could not even leave the inheritance of his ambitious projects to his son, the duke of Reichstadt, who grew up in Vienna under the guardianship of his grandfather, Emperor Francis I (II). The Congress of Vienna reinstated the principles of absolutism which the French revolution had shaken, and reproposed, at least in part, the territorial situation of 1790. For Austria this meant a position of predominion in northern and central Italy, thanks to the final acquisition of Lombardy and the Veneto and the fact that collateral lines of the Hapsburgs governed in Tuscany, Piacenza and Modena.

The "Italian" army thus became particularly important, that is the imperial army stationed in Italy, which represented about a third of the entire Hapsburg army. It demonstrated its worth in the campaigns of 1848-49, which were the result of the revolution which broke out in Vienna in March of 1848 and which were led by Radetzky. It was to him that Grillparzer dedicated the following words: "In your encampment is Austria". It expressed that sense of belonging to a single homeland shared by the soldiers who came from countries of the empire that were ethnically, economically, and

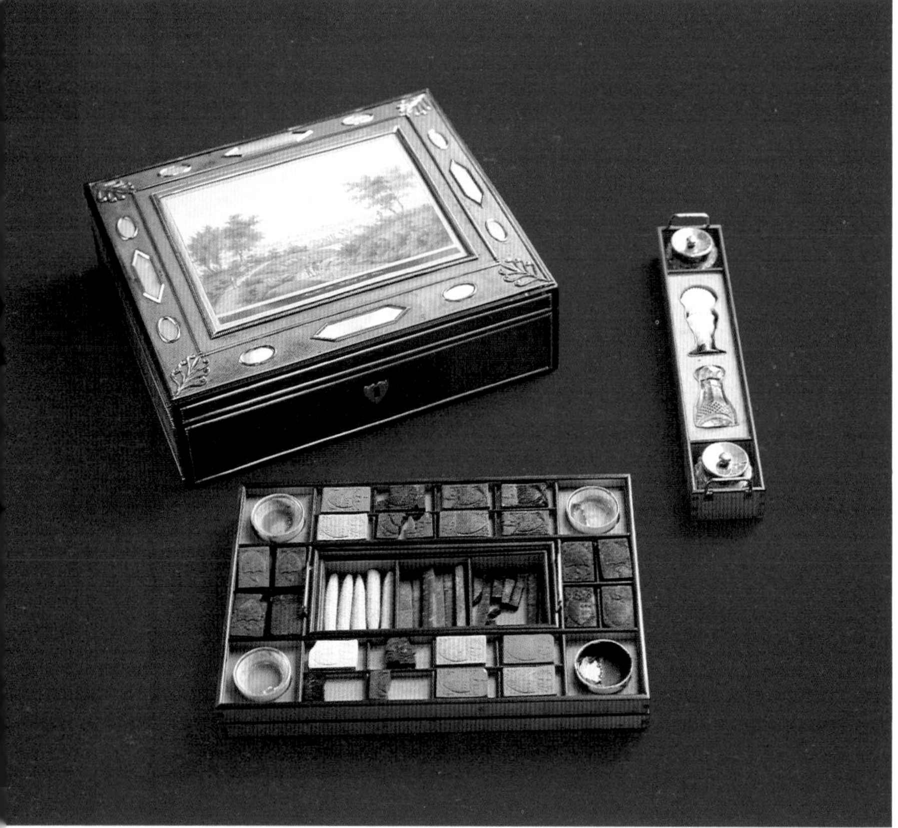

culturally different from each other. Radetzky Hall also contains the beaker of honor with which the "Italian" army thanked Grillparzer for his words.

The various colors of the uniforms in the first half of the 19th century and the close ties with civilian dress can be studied in the many original items as well as in the series of lithographs (at the time very popular) which depicted uniforms, and in the paintings.

In the second part of the hall the events of 1859, 1864 and 1866 are presented.

Austria could not long withstand the Italian attempts at national unification as a result of the movements of 1848: in the war jointly fought in 1859 by the Kingdom of Sardinia and France against Austria, the latter, after the defeats suffered at Magenta and Solferino (see p. 46), had to abandon Lombardy. At this time however the question of nationality dominated all of Europe. In 1846 Denmank too advanced claims on Schleswig-Holstein and in 1864 officially declared the annexation of Schleswig. This was successfully opposed by Austria and Prussia. The lieutenant general Baron Ludwig von Gablenz commanded the Austrian troops in this war and became governor of Holstein (the cup of honor given him by the emperor is on exhibition in this room). But the tensions between Austria and Prussia, a result of the joint administration of the duchy of Schleswig-Holstein, were aggravated in 1866 by the conflict for hegemony over Germany. Prussia, which had concluded a secret alliance with Italy of an offensive nature against Austria, asked that the latter be excluded from the German League. After the defeat of the main Austrian army, commanded by the army general Benedek at Sadowa (see p. 47), the German League was dissolved, Austria renounced the creation of a national German State, lost Venice, and in 1867 was forced to concede greater autonomy to the Hungarians.

Boy's uniform of the 4th Infantry regiment "Deutschmeister"

Worn during his military education, around 1843, by Archduke Francis Joseph, afterwards emperor as Francis Joseph I.

Flag of a battalion of an imperial infantry regiment

Painted yellow silk, 125 x 160 cm., pole 280 cm. According to the dispositions of 1836

In addition to the yellow flag of the battalion, each regiment carried a corps flag in white, with the Virgin Mary on one side and the two-headed eagle on the other.

Box of colors of the duke of Reichstadt (1811-1832)

Wood, ht., 7.1 cm.; width 25.4 cm., depth 22.2 cm.

On the lid, covered in leather and inlaid, a miniature by Balthasar Vigand (1771-1846), "View of Vienna", prior to 1820. In the compartments, English watercolors.

Dolman for generals in "Hungarian" uniform

Worn in 1848 by the lieutenant general Count Franz von Lamberg, who was killed on September 28, 1848 on the bridge of boats between Pest and Ofen.

Hussar's uniform (ca. 1848)

Blue Hussar style jacket for field officers of the Hussar regiment no. 4. The shako, rigid headgear with a visor used by the imperial army, originated in the 18th century from an ordinary felt cap of oriental origin. The "saber purse" was so called because it was hooked onto the saber and was used to carry documents. In Austria they were generally richly decorated with trimming and embroidery.

The taking of the Burgtor on October 31, 1848

FRANZ WERNER
Color lithograph printed in Vienna

After initial successes, the revolution that had broken out in Vienna on March 13, 1848 (in the wake of events in Paris) was suffocated by the army. On October 31, the imperial troops blew up the Burgtor and occupied the city. The state of siege proclaimed on October 22 was not revoked until 1853 by Emperor Francis Joseph I.

The Battle of Novara of May 23, 1894

ALBRECHT ADAM (1786-1862)
Oil on canvas, 120 x 175 cm. 1855

Field marshal Radetzky at the head of his staff, next to him the chief of staff Baron Heinrich von Hess. Von Hess's officers had this commemorative picture painted for the anniversary of his 50 years of service. In 1850 and 1854 Adam had painted the battle of Novara for Emperor Francis Joseph I and for King Louis I of Bavaria.

Field marshal Radetzky

GIOVANNI EMANUELI (1816-1894)
White marble, ht., 88.5 cm., 1854

Johann Joseph Franz Karl Radetzky, count of Radetz, imperial field marshal in 1836. In 1809 he was already general quartermaster and made the plans for the battle of Leipzig. As governor-general of the Kingdom of Lombardy-Venetia he succeeded in reforming the imperial army in Italy and obtained his major successes in 1848 and 1849. These victories were why the Viennese National Guard dedicated the saber of honor to him (designed by the architect Eduard van der Nüll), conferred in May 1849, in Milan. At the age of 91 Radetzky was still a commander of the army and a civilian and military governor-general. As a result of his request of December 17, 1856 to be discharged from service (above, left) the emperor exonerated him from service in February, 1857.

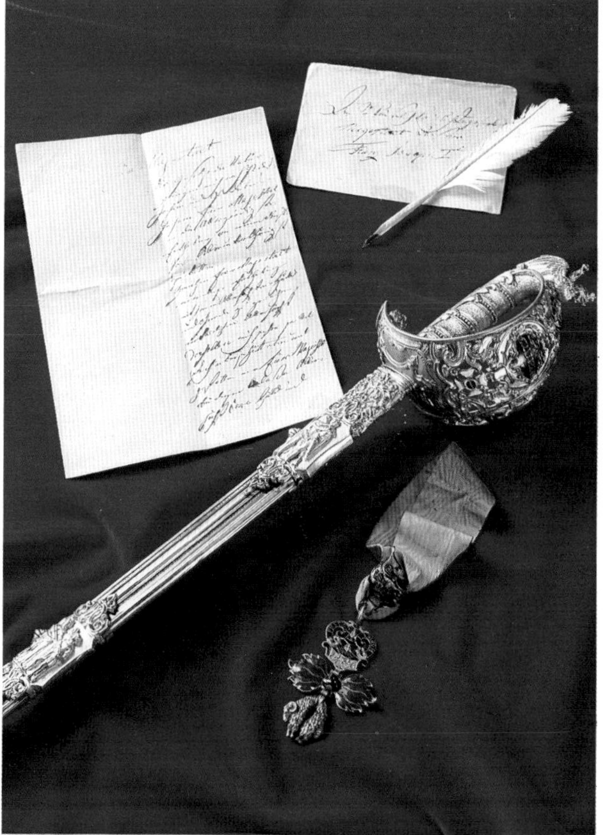

Field marshal Radetzky's saber of honor, the honor of the Golden Fleece and request for discharge

Transportation of the wounded after the battle of Solferino of June 24, 1859

HANS VON MAREES (1837-1887)
Oil on canvas, 41 x 51 cm., 1860

The defeat of Austria by the joint French and Piedmontese troops sealed the negative outcome of the war, which led to the loss of Lombardy. The high tribute in blood paid by both sides led to the Convention of Geneva and the founding of the Red Cross.

The artillery reserves of the army after the battle of Sadowa on July 3, 1866

CAVALIER RUDOLF OTTO VON OTTENFELD (1856-1913)
Oil on canvas, 194 x 289 cm., 1897

In the important battle of Sadowa (east of Prague) the artillery reserve covered the orderly retreat of the Austrian army, at a high cost. As soon as this picture had been painted it was called Death Battery (after a battery of the artillery reserve of the III army corps which was almost completely wiped out). In front of the picture: Austrian field cannon M 4-pounder (8 cm.) model of 1863. The piece is a muzzle-loader in bronze. The so-called "death battery" (cavalry battery no. 7/VIII) was equipped with arms of this type.

FROM 1867 TO 1914

The room on the ground floor to the right, also known as Francis Joseph Room, presents the period that goes from the compromise (Ausgleich) with Hungary (1867) to the attack at Sarajevo, in which period the Imperial Austrian army became the Hungarian Austrian army. This period of peace, which lasted more than half a century, in the course of which Austria, after having been defeated in the war of 1866 against Prussia, turned its attention to the Balkans, was interrupted only by the occupation of Bosnia and Herzegovinia in 1878. In 1908 these territories were annexed and this was one of the reasons for World War I. This was the epoch of generalized obligatory conscription, the transformation of the territorial militias, and a recognition of the importance of the progress of technical knowledge in the military field. Some of the showcases in the room are dedicated to the transformation of the uniform, from the "many-colored" dress of the 19th century to the ever more homogeneous colors of the eve of World War I. Others present the technical innovations of photography, the telephone, aviation and the automobile, and their development between the end of the 19th and the beginning of the 20th century. Even so the importance of Lieutenant Günther Burstyn's invention was not immediately recognized nor appreciated when, as early as 1911, he designed an armored tank of which a model is exhibited. The alert visitor will take note of the ethnic and cultural variety of the great Hapsburgic empire, transformed into a constitutional monarchy by Emperor Francis Joseph I, not only in the formulas of the oath of allegiance to the flag, in all of eleven different languages, and in the so-called "Palette of colors" (that is the enormous variety of tints and hues in the banners of each of the 102 regiments of the imperial infantry and other troops), but also in a rich series of photographs by Oskar Brüch, made for the Budapest Exposition of 1896 (which celebrated the millenary of Hungary), showing all the types and "branches" of the troops, from the teamsters of the stud farms for the renewal of the Puszta cavalry to the army chaplains.
The social importance of the army, which also produced many scholars, poets and artists, clearly emerges from the numerous pieces exhibited. The figure of the emperor Francis Joseph has become the symbol of the multinational state. An entire showcase has been reserved for this sovereign who was true to duty and who lived an extremely simple life. His long reign (1848-1916) was saddened by the death of his son Rudolf in 1889

(see p. 50), the assassination of his consort the empress Elisabeth ("Sissi") in 1898, and the assassination of the heir to the throne, Archduke Francis Ferdinand, friend of the Slavs and married to a Bohemian countess, in 1914. A separate area is dedicated to this last event which set off World War I, thus closing the chronological representation of the history of "old Austria".
In the subsequent rooms specific displays present paintings of World War I or other themes of contemporary epoch up to the current federal army of Austria.

Uniforms of Emperor Francis Joseph I

Next to his field marshal's coat (blue-grey campaign coat with hat and white gala coat with dome-shaped hat) is the emperor's house coat (on the left) (a shortened general's coat).

Emperor Francis Joseph I (1830-1916)

FRIEDRICH FRANCESCHINI (1845-1906)
Oil on canvas, 73.5 x 60 cm., 1875

The painting shows the 45-year old emperor in his gala uniform of field marshal with the white jacket.

Mementos of Archduke Rudolf

Next to the arms and the hats worn by Archduke Rudolf (1858-1889) is a revolver caliber 9 mm. dedicated to him by the Firm Gasser. The heir to the throne was to have participated in a meeting of the board of directors of the Army Museum on January 29, 1889. The open guestbook shows that Rudolf did not show up. On January 30th he committed suicide at Mayerling.

Archduke Francis Ferdinand of Austria-Este (1863-1914)

KASIMIERSK POCHWALSKI (1855-1940)
Oil on canvas, 68 x 55.5 cm., unfinished, 1914

After the death of the hereditary prince Rudolf, the archduke Francis Ferdinand became the successor to the throne. In 1913 Emperor Francis Joseph had already nominated him "Inspector General of all the armed forces", thus to all extents ceding him the supreme command in times of peace. Francis Ferdinand was killed on June 28, 1914 at Sarajevo by a Serbian nationalist.

Uniform of Archduke Francis Ferdinand

General's jacket and hat and blue-gray trousers worn on June 28, 1914 at Sarajevo.

The automobile of the heir to the throne

The archduke Francis Ferdinand and his wife, the duchess Sophie von Hohenberg, were riding through Sarajevo in this Gräf and Stift auto (built in 1910, 4 cylinders, 28/32 H.P.) when they were hit by the mortal bullets from the Browning 9 mm. pistol of the assassin Gavrilo Princip.

Mementos of the campaign of the occupation of Bosnia-Herzegovina in 1878

Banner taken from the rebels, and oriental arms; on the right, uniforms and arms that belonged to general Baron Josef von Philippovic (1818-1889) who commanded the occupation army

Helmet of the mounted body guard, model 1878-1898.

Embossed sheet silver, ht., 28.5 cm.

The two-headed eagle at the top, the projecting band, coats of arms and decorations in gilded bronze are partially hidden by the plume in white buffalo hair.

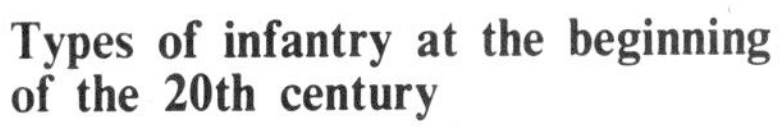

Types of infantry at the beginning of the 20th century

LUDWIG KOCH (1866-1934)
Watercolor, 1901

Left to right: foot soldier of the Fourth infantry regiment of Bosnia-Herzegovina; lieutenant of the Fifth infantry regiment of the territorial militia; standard bearer sergeant of the Fourth infantry regiment.

Body guard of Emperor Francis Joseph

Uniform of the noble Hungarian body guard (on the left); (on the right) uniform of the first mounted body guard.

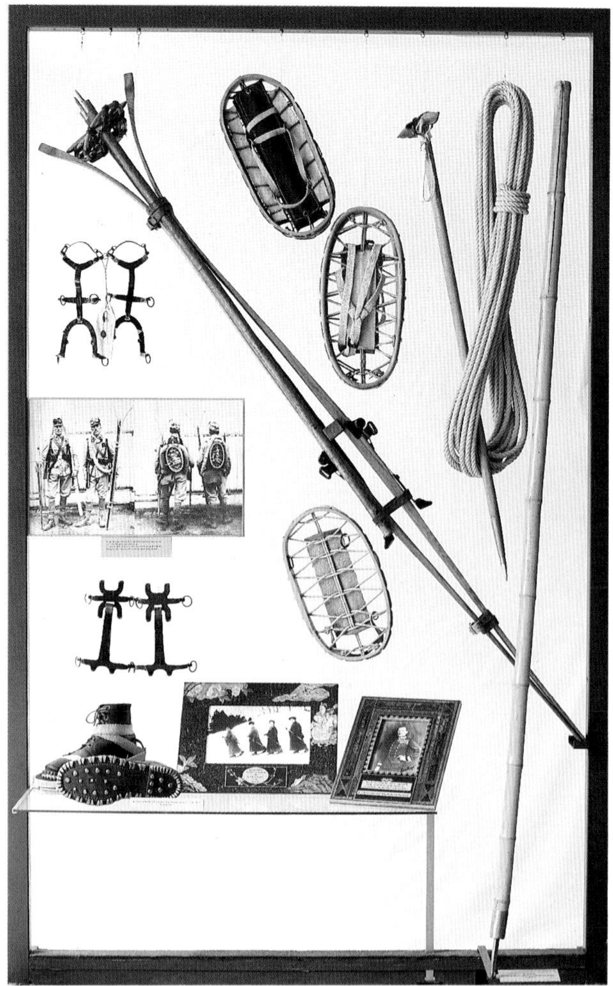

Military balloon, model 1896

Scale model, 1:20

Exhibited underneath are models (in 1:10 scale) of the "Etrich-Taube" A II and a biplane Lohner type B.

Mountain equipment for the Alpine troops

As early as 1906 the first troops for high mountain fighting were created within the imperial army.

Machine gun, model 1907 Schwarzlose system

Caliber 8 mm.

This modern machine gun was used in World War I and by the Federal army of the First Austrian Republic up to 1938. This weapon, which fell into Italian hands in great number at the end of the war of 1915-1918, was used by the Italian colonial troops and the Royal African Troops in the colonies.

HEAVY ARTILLERY HALL

With its enormous pieces, this room clearly illustrates how the technical evolution touched on in the preceding pages necessarily led to larger, heavier, more efficient weapons. From bronze muzzle-loading cannons and the coastal cannons of the last three decades of the 19th century, used in defending the Austro-Hungarian coasts of the Adriatic, to the anti-aircraft artillery and an automatic cannon of World War I, up to the enormous 38 cm. howitzer, a masterpiece of technology, which was the last piece of artillery built and used by the Austro-Hungarian army during World War I.
German artillery had shown its worth in the war of 1866, but proved inferior in range and firing velocity to that of the other European powers. The decisive leap took place in World War I. Trench warfare required artillery that was more efficient and in 1914-17 seven types were developed, including the 38 cm. howitzer mentioned above. That such powerful artillery was a menace to fixed fortifications (which had been increasingly fortified since the beginning of the 20th century) is demonstrated by examples of steel domes dating to World War I. The penetration power of the Austrian grenades of 30.5 cm. was tested on a strong armed plaque 30 cm. thick, which corresponded technically to the construction material used in the armored plates of the British men of war. Sad to say, the Heeresgeschichtliches Museum no longer has even one example of the legendary 30.5 cm. mortar which launched these grenades. The example exhibited in 1934 in the mortar room of the museum was transferred by the supreme command of the German Wehrmacht during World War II to the Russian front and since then it has been missing. The oldest pieces of artillery - with bronze guns and dating to the 17th and 18th centuries, in part richly

38 cm mortar, model 1916

Built by the Skoda Works of Pilsen; 1916-17

Modern piece of artillery with a recoil barrel, range 15 km., weight 81,000 kg.

decorated - are exhibited outside the museum, under the porticoes and in the garden. They date to an epoch in which artillery was still organized and managed as an autonomous corporation. After the middle of the 18th century, thanks to the reforms of General Joseph Wenzel prince of Liechtenstein, it was transformed into one of the branches of the army.

Armored dome, 8 cm., model 1894

It belonged to posting 1/2 of the Przenysi fortress (Galitia); hit on the mark by a Russian 25 cm. mortar shot.

"To the Unknown Soldier 1914"

ALBIN EGGER LIENZ (1868-1926)
Tempera on canvas, 245 x 476 cm., 1916

In this picture the Tyrolean artist created one of the most famous historical paintings of the 20th century, a picture which became a symbol of modern mass warfare.

Automatic 15 cm. cannon, model 1915 (at the center); plate from an armor belt for a warship, 1913 (left); armored dome of fort Kessel near Antwerp (right).

The cannon has a range of 20.7 km. The dome was destroyed in the autumn of 1914 by a shot from an Austro-Hungarian 30.5 cm. mortar.

NAVY HALL

This room reminds the visitor that up to 1918 the Hapsburg empire was an important maritime power and had a powerful military navy as well as a fleet of merchant ships.
Models of ships, flags, equipment and numerous pictures give an insight into the important periods and personages of Austrian naval history.
The visitor can observe the development of the Austrian navy from the first examples of "Danubian barges" (flat armed river boats, used for supplies) employed in the war against the Turks in the 17th century, up to the passage of wooden sailing ships and the armored steam boats of the second half of the 19th century. The invention of the imperial frigate captian Johann Blasius Luppis, who tried to create a teleguided mine layer for the defense of the coasts, led to the first torpedoboat, which Luppis developed at Fiume in the shipyards of the Englishman, Robert Whitehead, beginning in 1866. The Whitehead torpedoboat permitted an efficacious wartime use of submarines (which were also invented at the middle of the 19th century). In 1906 the Austro-Hungarian empire introduced submarines in its navy.
The technical evolution also led to innovations in artillery used on warships as well, such as those realized in the class "Viribus Unitis".
The political-cultural or scientific feats of the Austrian fleet are recorded in this hall as well as the wartime use in 1864 (Helgoland) and 1866 (Lissa). The circumnavigation of the globe by the frigate "Novara" in 1857-59, guided by the future emperor Maximilian of Mexico, is illustrated by numerous works by the painter Joseph Selleny. The expedition to the North Pole of 1872-74, financed by the great maecenas Hans Wilczek, is documented above all by a model of the research ship "Admiral Tegetthoff" and by photos of the participants, as well as the diary, drawings and paintings of the artist and naval officer, Julius von Payer.
A striking document of the employment of the navy in World War I is the tower of command of the Austrian submarine no. 20, sunk in 1918. The display also deals with the naval air forces and the employment of airborne troops in World War I, as well as the aerial equipment of the federal Austrian army in the First and Second Republic.

Archduke Ferdinand Maximilian (1832-1867)

GEORG DECKER (1819-1894)
Pastel on cardboard, 81.1 x 65.5 cm. ca. 1857

Archduke Ferdinand Maximilian, younger brother of Emperor Francis Joseph, rear admiral and navy commander in 1854, reformed the Austrian navy and in 1857 became governor-general of Lombardy-Venetia. In 1864 he was given the crown of Emperor of Mexico and on June 19, 1867 he was assassinated in Queretaro.

The frigate "Novara"

Model in 1:75 scale

The frigate was built in Venice in 1850 and transformed into a propellor frigate in 1861-62. In 1857-59 it circumnavigated the globe. In 1867 the ship brought the mortal remains of Emperor Maximilian of Mexico back to Europe.

Vice Admiral Wilhelm von Tegetthof (1827-1871)

GEORG DECKER (1819-1894)
Pastel on cardboard, 88 x 73 cm., after 1866

Tegetthof distinguished himself as early as the German-Danish war, in the naval battle of 1864 in front of Helgoland, and became famous for his victory near the Adriatic island of Lissa. As naval commander he tried to increase the shock force of the fleet.

The naval battle of Lissa on July 20, 1866

CARL FREDERIK SORENSEN (1818-1879)
Oil on canvas, 84 x 120.5 cm., 1868

The Austrian flagship "Ferdinand Max" rammed the Italian battleship "Re d'Italia" and sank it. Thanks to his superior tactics, Tegetthoff managed to win despite the fact that he disposed of inferior forces.

Gift of honor presented by the city of Trieste to Wilhelm von Tegetthoff

MAYERHOFER & KLINKOSCH court goldsmiths of Vienna (design by Volker), 1867

The statuettes of Naval Construction, Navigation, Commerce and Industry symbolize the importance of the port and mercantile city of Trieste, the safety of which was guaranteed by Tegetthoff's victory at Lissa. The warship held aloft by the Triton represents the frigate "Ferdinand Max", Tegetthoff's flagship.

Ever Onwards

JULIUS VON PAYER (1842-1915)
Oil on canvas, 324.5 x 459 cm., 1892

In this monumental painting Julius von Payer, who took part in the Austro-Hungarian expedition to the North Pole in 1872-74, represents the moment when the men had to leave the ship and begin their march on ice. The principal scientific result of this research expedition of the imperial navy was the discovery of Francis Joseph Land (ca. 80° north latitude).

His Majesty's warship "Viribus Unitis"

Model, cross section, scale 1:25

The "Viribus Unitis", last flagship of the Austro-Hungarian navy, was launched in 1911. Ships of this class were characterized by twelve 30.5 cm. cannons in four three-gun turrets. Two officers of the Italian navy, Raffaele Rossetti and Raffaele Paolucci, sank the ship on November 1, 1918 in the port of Pola after the imperial fleet had been ceded to Yugoslavia.

Turret of the Hapsburg U-20 submarine

This submarine, built in 1917, was sunk by an Italian warship in 1918 at the mouth of the Tagliamento and not recuperated until 1962. The command turrets and the survivors of the crew were sent back to Austria.

Biplane Albatros B (prototype)

Wingspread 13 m., length 7.6 m.

This training and reconnaisance biplane was built in 1914 as a prototype in the Albatros factory. The fusillage was made in Berlin while the wing surfaces were manufactured in Vienna.

General view of the tank park

The armored vehicles used in the Austrian army from 1955 on are on exhibit here. Some of them belonged to the ex-occupation forces. From right to left: armored car M-8 (USA) used from 1959 to 1968; light battle tank M-24 (USA), used from 1955 to 1968; medium battle tank T-34 (85) (URSS), used from 1955 to 1964; armored light howitzer M-7B2 (USA) used from 1961 to 1979.

BESTEIGEN
DER PANZER
IST
VERBOTEN!

Thousand pound mortar

Made of metal bars, length 258 cm., diam. gun 88 cm. (caliber 80 cm.), weight 7,100 kg.

Styria, first half of the 15th century. This ancient piece of artillery from the imperial arsenal in Vienna is one of the few late-medieval pieces of large size that have come down to us. Its range must have been about 600 meters.

Demi cannon nicknamed "Singerin"

MARTIN II HILGER (1538-1601)

Cast bronze, overall length 344 cm., caliber 16 cm., 1579. Detail of the cannon which took its name from a songbird represented on the central part; on the reverse is an old bearded Turk.

The "culverins of the months of Nuremberg"

JOHANN BALTHASAR HEROLD (documented 1693-1726)

Cast bronze, overall length 251 cm., caliber 7.8 cm., weight 682 kg., 1708.
These twelve culverins of three pounds each, bear the coats of arms of the Nuremberg nobles Volckamer, Harsdörfer, Tucher and Schlüsselfelder, and each one a symbol in relief and the name of a month. They reached the arsenal in 1864 from the imperial country castle of Laxenburg.